Published by 31*st* and Seventh Publishing, LLC,

a subsidiary of 3.1.7 Media

Port Orange, FL 32128

Copyright © 2012 by Jon Marc Creighton

Bona fide Fool: Perhaps Yesterday but Definitely not Today

Includes References

ISBN-10: 0990453723
ISBN-13: 978-0-9904537-2-7

Hard Copy Printed in the United States of America

Fool: You're Being Played Like a Fiddle.
The "Wool" is Being Blatantly Pulled Over Your Eyes!
And Here's Why…

Preamble

Not Your Typical "Blah-Blah-Blah, I've Heard It All Before" Mainstream Book

If you were expecting or counting on settling back, relaxing and half-heartedly breezing through another nice, jovial or feel-good book, then I am sorry to disappoint you. Conversely, the strong content and words assembled in this book will actually require a tremendous amount of effort and analytical thinking on your part, particularly when it comes down to reasoning, drawing concise conclusions and making wise intelligent decisions.

To ensure that we are all on the same page or cadence, I'd like to repeat that last entire sentence. "Conversely, the strong content and words assembled in this book will actually require a tremendous amount of effort and analytical thinking on your part, particularly when it comes down to reasoning, drawing concise conclusions and making wise intelligent decisions."

With that being duly noted and clarified right up front, your first assignment is to grab an ink pen and begin underlining the following words Effort and Analytical Thinking. Once that is accomplished, go ahead and highlight or underline the words

Reasoning, <u>Drawing concise Conclusions</u> and <u>Making wise Intelligent Decisions</u>.

… and here's why We will be referring back to these five thought-provoking components and concepts throughout the entire book, so having them clearly marked will not only help magnify their importance, but will serve as a quick reminder of their progressive and strategic sequence.

1 Effort, 2 Analytical Thinking, 3 Reasoning, 4 Drawing concise Conclusions, 5 Making wise Intelligent Decisions

Now as tempting as it may be, I am going to ask that you do not rush through or jump ahead of any of these five components from this proven, well-tested winning-formula because when it's all said and done, it's going to be the summation of one through five that will solidify and validate why <u>Professionalism</u> is vastly "over-stated / over-rated" or why <u>People Skills</u> are cleverly "disguised / distorted" and why <u>Priorities</u> are so scornfully "under-utilized / and have gone amiss."

At this time, I would be remiss if I didn't offer a word of caution; the winning-formula mentioned above is not for the weary, faint or weak-hearted. But rather it's designed intently and purposefully for those individuals who are truly committed, dedicated and interested in becoming a much stronger, wiser, more vibrant leader in the things they do and say. Plus, these five components are exclusively engineered for those wanting to make wise intelligent decisions, one right after the other, back to back, morning, noon and night.

However, if you are still totally hell bent on remaining cynical, skeptical and hard-headed, then perhaps now is the best time for you to simply toss this book aside, because the rest of us are going to aggressively dissect and delve into each of these five components**. ... and here's why** It's imperative, before moving any further, that we grasp with accurate certainty how each of these components operate independently and separately of one another, yet fully recognizing their added strength or synergy when they finally do connect, perform and function in total unison.

The specific task of retaining this winning-formula is pinnacle and essential, so a practical way to help remember the five major components is to literally think of them as five distinctive, crystal clear musical notes. By that I mean, when you strike or play a single note on an instrument, it's soothing and sounds okay. But it's only after you learn how to string together several notes at a time that you suddenly realize or discover, "Wow! I can't believe it; I am actually making beautiful music."

This electrifying phenomenon doesn't just happen overnight. It takes hours, weeks and months of obtaining, absorbing and securing the necessary information and knowledge to reach such a musical plateau.

Yesterday, it was nothing more than just a worn-down, dusty old piano sitting over in the corner, but today, I am now capable of transforming all 88 of those tiny little keys into something worthwhile and meaningful. Now, I am not suggesting that everyone needs to run out and begin taking piano lessons in order to achieve success, but I am going to stand firm behind the basic principle that listening, learning and applying what you have been taught will lead you to that higher level of success. Extraordinary.

Each semester, aspiring music students will inquisitively ask this astounding question "How do you get to Carnegie Hall? Well, the most direct, popular and honest answer is always recited in this fashion: practice, practice and practice. Ironically, this same advice holds true for the three sections of this book, Professionalism, People Skills and Priorities.

I

<u>PROFESSIONALISM</u>
Vastly Over-Rated/Over-Stated

Upon glancing over the five components, you may be wondering to yourself, why in the world wouldn't "ENTHUSIASM" be selected or chosen? Well, my friend, you bring up a valid and interesting point. For all intents and purposes, "Enthusiasm" is one of those awesome traits that is admired by many. As a matter of fact, I can assure you, I absolutely love being around those who are enthusiastic. They are so contagious and most of all, it's so true what they say: "Enthusiasm does breed Enthusiasm." However, I'd like for you to pause for a moment and ponder this very point. Just because someone appears to be highly enthusiastic or somewhat excited about a particular subject matter, it doesn't mean, that same individual has put forth the necessary time and energy needed to earn his so-called stripes.

Take for example the art of playing golf. It's one thing to be highly enthusiastic, perhaps joking a bit or even in jest, detailing how many "birdies" will be falling throughout your round, but it's an entirely different ball game to consistently put yourself in a position, near or up on the green, to give yourself a legitimate opportunity to attempt a "birdie" putt. So jump and shout all you want, but unless you are willing to put forth the extra "EFFORT" and practice countless hours on your short game, all that excitement and high energy being displayed might be done for naught. Please do not misunderstand what I am trying to convey or communicate here, because there is definitely merit and value added by bringing high energy and enthusiasm to the table. Often times "Enthusiasm" will tip the scale towards your advantage. However, in order to achieve long-lasting, sustainable and consistent results in major projects or personal relationships, I'll choose "EFFORT" as our point of entry.

EFFORT

The first component that we must all embrace and wrap our arms around is this thing called "EFFORT" or unfortunately, the lack of it.

If you would, take a moment and allow yourself to slowly, gently drift back to an earlier time in your life, perhaps as far back as high school or maybe even middle school. Are you approaching that era yet? Okay, let me ask you, do you recall ever hearing one of your favorite teachers or energetic coaches giving one of their inspiring, heartfelt speeches involving "EFFORT?" Well, if they were loud, vocal or animated as I distinctively remember mine being, then I bet their rendition sounded something like this: "EFFORT" will ultimately define one's desire, drive or motivation towards accomplishing lofty goals or objectives. In other words, the amount of "EFFORT" one is willing to put forth will more than likely determine whether that individual turns out highly successful or not.

It's so ironic, but this word "EFFORT" is so often associated with another word called "Work" that it's quickly ignored and brushed aside. This is really quite sad, because "EFFORT" and work even though they may appear and sound similar, are actually quite different from one another.

... and here's why

Take for example, the art of changing dirty diapers. Is it strenuous work or simply an honest act of human kindness? Changing dirty diapers in my opinion should never, ever, ever be called or classified as hard work, especially when you pause long enough to ponder the positive end-results of what you are truly hoping to accomplish by performing this task.

Once again, because this phrase is so profound and truly captures the overall premise of this book, I'd like for you to go ahead and highlight or underline the entire sentence. *"Changing dirty diapers should never, ever,ever be called or classified as hard work, especially when you pause long enough to ponder the positive end-results of what you are truly hoping to accomplish or want to achieve by performing this task."*

Seriously, think about this concept for a moment. When you and I physically go through the normal and proper steps of changing a dirty diaper, we are actually assisting a helpless, tiny infant by removing irritating feces from his soft, sensitive skin. So tell me, how in the world can grabbing a clean diaper, a few wet-wipes and some baby powder be misconstrued or called strenuous work, when in reality it's nothing more than a pure dose of "EFFORT?"

So my friend let me ask you, at this particular point in your life is "EFFORT" even remotely showing up on your personal radar screen? Are there lofty or legitimate goals you know you need to be actively pursuing or are you just content with sitting idly by glued to the couch not accomplishing squat?

So perhaps "Effort" is worth pursuing.

ANALYTICAL THINKING

Without a doubt, component two, "Analytical Thinking" is probably the most frightening and scary of all five concepts. With that being said, that's precisely why so many of your closest family and friends are so quick to shy away from this very component, because it sounds like it might involve some math. How many times have you heard, "Well now, if it has anything to do with calculating numbers, finding percentages or figuring out fancy formulas, then just count me out."

This typical response or mindset is somewhat disturbing and troubling, because in actuality, studying and analyzing solid numbers is not that difficult of a task to accomplish or even excel in. No kidding, you will be shocked, amazed and totally blown away by discovering and learning what certain numbers are indicating and what they are exactly trying to tell you**. ... and here's why**

Take for example, this every day, basic equation, 7+ 7. Now, it appears pretty simple and straight forward. However, before jumping up and down, eager or excited to blurt out the answer that 7 + 7 always equals 14, I'd like for you to slow down, pause for a brief moment, just long enough to ponder the end-results. In other words, what does that number seven actually represent? Is it truly reliable or trustworthy? Based upon your investigation, research or findings, are you 100% certain that you know exactly without a shadow of a doubt where that number seven generated from? Does that number seven mean you are talking about the 7th inning stretch or 7 seconds remaining in a closely contested ballgame? Perhaps you misheard or misunderstood and that number seven actually represents 7 hours before tip-off. There's no possibility of that number seven referring to 7 disgruntled fans, employees or 7 extremely nervous board members? So you can easily see why it's crucial that you know exactly what these numbers are indicating. My friend, it's your responsibility—not Main Street or the social media outlets—to interpret or sort through these numbers for you. You must be the one drilling down and taking charge on sorting through the accurate data and research laid squarely in your lap.

From this day forward, "Analytical Thinking" does not have to be a painful experience or dreaded chore. Once you've learned the key to actually implementing this vital step of "Analytical Thinking" into your daily routine and thought process, you will begin saving hundreds, if not thousands of dollars.

So perhaps "Analytical Thinking" is worth pursuing.

REASONING

It's intriguing and literally amazing the number of people who ass/u/me "Reasoning" will be the easiest of all five components to figure out, maneuver and start utilizing; however, that's just not the case.

As living, breathing, creatures of our habits, we are notorious even predictable for getting the terminology of "Reasoning" and "Common Sense" all mixed up. These two terms "Reasoning" and

"Common Sense" are not even in the same ball park. **... and here's why**

Take for example the art of driving a motorized vehicle. "Common Sense" will tell you that you need two hands to safely maneuver and operate a steering wheel, but look closely into the trucks and automobiles next to you and you will observe drivers smoking cigarettes in one hand, trying to put on eye liner with the other, while creatively attempting to press their hand-held electronic device up against their head and shoulders.

Every once in a while you come across that sophisticated driver who thinks there is absolutely nothing wrong with allowing a small furry pet to rest its cute little head upon her left arm or shoulder while attempting to turn a vehicle in heavy traffic. So, please don't ass/u/me that common sense and reasoning are one and the same. Obviously they are not. There is a profound difference.

"Reasoning" requires the ability to "interpret" our innermost desires, cravings and urges. It's like our own internal filtering system which can sort through all of the possible consequences that might occur emotionally, physically and mentally if we proceed to   go ahead and act upon our cravings or urges. "Reasoning" takes courage to fully grasp. It involves logic and a willingness to pause long enough to ponder some tough questions throughout our busy and hectic day.

Ever wonder why the Master Carpenter might deliberately instruct you to measure twice, before cutting once? Is that a voice of "Reason" or a voice of experience and logic? Perhaps his insight and wisdom of suggesting that you take a little extra time to measure a second time, prior to you just ripping through that board, might just save and prevent you from making a costly mistake.

So perhaps "Reasoning" is worth pursuing.

DRAWING concise CONCLUSIONS

Component four of our winning-formula can be extremely difficult and tough to manage. The main objective is to seek and rescue the entire truth. Drawing concise Conclusions is the ability to collect and pull together all the necessary or pertinent data from reliable or legitimate sources, rather than just cow tailing or basing your decisions on pure rumor or popular opinion.

If you are not cautious, the fancy rhetoric and hearsay will have you bouncing in all sorts of directions. But keep in mind, our goal is to obtain the entire truth.

Take, for example, the scientific discussion surrounding the basic physics of gravity; some scholars may claim that you must refer to it as the "Law" of gravity, whereas another group of experts may scream that you refer to it as the "Force of gravity."

The bottom line is this, if you drop a sixteen pound bowling ball and a tiny golf ball from a roof top of let's say fifteen feet, both of these objects will land at the same time. Granted, seeking the truth may leave you scratching your forehead, but the thing you must always remember is, it's ok to conduct some research and eliminate the gray areas.

In this fast paced, high tech information age we are living in, it's imperative that "You" can distinguish fluff from facts or recognize the difference between style and substance.

 Take the following two options for example. Which one provides you personally with the most depth and clarity?

Assuming things will get done" or "Accurately knowing that things got done?"

Take your time; there's no need to rush, just be certain of your answer. Notice how you were able to formulate your thoughts without the help or hounding influence or pressure from the far left or extreme right. Notice, "You" were capable of using your talents, skills and abilities to surmise and seek out the truth. If you can, retrieve that ink pen or marker we used earlier to highlight or underline, the phrase "formulate your thoughts" in this paragraph.

So perhaps "Drawing concise Conclusions" is worth pursuing.

MAKING wise INTELLIGENT DECISIONS

Hopefully, that ink pen or highlighter is still within reach. If you will, retrieve it and completely underline or highlight the following subtitle of this book, which says; "Perhaps yesterday, but definitely not today." **... and here's why**

Everyone, including myself has unfortunately made several poor, damaging and devastating life choices. Often times, these decisions have turned out to be extremely painful, bitter, sour and quite pun gent. However, do not become overwhelmed, disenchanted or even frustrated, because the premise behind this book is not for us to wallow in our past failures and flaws, but rather to focus on the necessary tools that can prevent us from making the same old mistakes over and over again.

One of my favorite analogies that I tend to use quite often goes like this: "Just because one little egg happens to roll off the kitchen counter, smashing to the floor, doesn't mean that the entire recipe or scheduled celebration has to be completely ruined." In other words, if we are willing to own up to our mistakes and learn from them, the sooner we will discover we can actually prevent other eggs from rolling off the counter. It pays to learn from our mistakes.

Coach Robert Montgomery Knight and Coach Mike Krzyzewski are prime examples of the value and merit behind this principle.

Winning eight national titles in men's college basketball is a tall mountain to climb; however, Coach Knight and Coach Krzyzewski collectively have achieved this amazing plateau during their coaching careers. Both of these remarkable coaches were dedicated to instructing, encouraging and teaching their players respectively the sustaining value behind eliminating turnovers and mistakes. It stands to reason that every time you make an errant or terrible pass, you are basically giving your opponent the ball right back, with the opportunity to go down court and score on you, so by eliminating your mistakes you will actually increase your chances or percentages for winning games.

Research has shown that there is a common thread or major attribute among sustaining and excellent leaders. Without question, they all possess a keen sense of responsibility for those around them. Instinctively, they seem to have a knack for understanding the importance of reaching down and helping others achieve the same—if not more—success, than they have experienced themselves. The proof is definitely in the pudding. In 1966, Mike Krzyzewski was a basketball player under Coach Bob Knight at West Point Military Academy. After graduating, Mike began his coaching career. Some 45 years later in 2011, Coach Mike Krzyzewski surpassed his mentor, friend and teacher as the all-time winningest coach in the history of men's major college basketball with

903 career wins. Coach Knight retired from coaching in 2008 with 902 career wins.

Take a moment, Pause and Ponder. Look around you; is there someone standing well within your midst that could benefit from you as a solid mentor?

The profound difference between winning and losing actually comes down to making fewer mistakes both on and off the court and your ability to make wise intelligent decisions.

So perhaps "Making wise Intelligent Decisions" is worth pursuing.

DOUBLE-ORDER OF HASH BROWNS:

Hot / Delicious - Quantifiable / Tangible

Let's suppose one morning, while you and I were enjoying a nice cup of coffee at our favorite breakfast spot, I casually turned to our server and asked for two eggs over easy with a delicious double-order of hash browns on the side. Would you in any way find that request to be all that unusual or out of the ordinary?

I mean come on now; ordering a double-portion of hash browns is as normal as it gets. It's authentic, straight forward and easy to follow. You simply locate the right person to make your desires and wishes known, while ensuring all along that you are stating your request in a clear, precise and well-defined manner. Then, it's just a matter of waiting patiently for your delicious order of two eggs over easy with a double-portion of hash browns to be delivered to your table.

I merely mention the above scenario, because it's something to which we can all relate. It illustrates with such ease, just how simplistic our requests and expectations can be at times. For example, you and I can easily surmise just by glancing down at the plate, if the end-result— again, what we are hoping for and expecting— precisely meet or match our request. Seriously, there's no need to call for a special panel or create a task force to wait for them to provide us an answer.

We can actually determine if there is a single scoop or a double portion of hash browns sitting on our plate. You and I are quite capable of quantifying and measuring the end-results for ourselves.

Okay, now sticking with this same scenario, but this time around, I'll turn towards the fine folks sitting in the booth next to ours and ask for some "Professionalism." Would this simple request change or alter your expectations in any way?

Very much like before, the question I presented is totally direct and to the point. In fact, it's clear and precise. Where things seem to get fuzzy and start falling apart, however, involves that third and final piece to our question, and that is, was our request well-defined or even understood?

Remember, back in the first scenario, our hot and delicious hash browns were measurable and tangible; however, in the second scenario, there's not a whole lot that we can sink our teeth into. They appear complicated, confusing and complex.

The pure manner in which all these responses are being blurted out or tossed around clearly illustrates that "Professionalism" is not well-defined or understood. The opinions are somewhat "scattered, smothered and covered."

In plain simple terms, the positive end-results of what we hope for or expect concerning "Professionalism" are just not as cut and dry as ordering a double-portion of hash browns**. ... and here's why**

Even though all the formal scholastic dictionaries can eloquently describe the word "Professionalism," it still is an unknown entity. It operates under a wide range of meanings, interpretations and unwritten rules. It's vague, and loosie-goosie. You see, no one wants to admit it, but the term "Professionalism" has never, ever been officially adopted or publically clarified in a broad spectrum. In fact, very few occupations provide a formal proclamation.

Let me ask you a very important question. Have you or anyone in your immediate family or perhaps organization ever received a degree or certificate in "Professionalism?"

Everyone walks around assuming that it's basically understood and needs no explanation. But the bottom line is this, is "Professionalism" defined by the clothes you wear? Perhaps it's defined by your DNA or blood type? Does "Professionalism" happen before or after eating breakfast?

No one knows for certain what "Professionalism" is supposed to look or feel like. Is "Professionalism" based solely upon one's age, gender or wealth?

Do you think "Professionalism" has anything to do with your judgment, demeanor or leadership style? Do you think the persona of "Professionalism" begins the moment you leave your driveway or is it something that can wait until you arrive or reach your point of destination? Perhaps, the mindset of "Professionalism" actually kicks in three or four traffic lights just prior to the estimated time of arrival? No one knows for sure what "Professionalism" is supposed to encompass.

I do realize this book alone may not alter the course of our modern society, but I hope it might finally define and set some parameters surrounding this incredible word we like to call "professionalism" once and for all. The following illustration might just shed some light on what constitutes "Professionalism" in our daily lives.

Mirrors: In Spite Of All The Smudges   Still Significant / Monumental

Okay leading experts, why do photons, particles of light bounce off an object or person, absorbed by electrons, which then emit a reflection? What could possibly be the value added behind these tiny pieces of glass? Have you ever paused long enough to ponder why humans glance at themselves in a mirror? What could possibly be the positive end-results of doing something like this? What do we want to accomplish or hope to achieve by spending a few minutes looking at ourselves in a mirror?

Sometime today or tomorrow, I'd like for you to physically go and locate a mirror that you feel most comfortable with, preferably the one you use every morning or evening, because it's probably the one true mirror that has actually seen you at the best and worst of times. However, before getting all wrapped up in checking out your own facial portrait, I'd like for you to take a moment and notice the finer details surrounding this mirror you have chosen. Is it oval or rectangular? Does it have beveled edges? Is it in a wooden frame? The point I am trying to make here, is that often times we are in such a rush when we are standing in the mirror, clearly focused on the task at hand, checking out how we look, that we overlook and let things go unnoticed. Yesterday has come and gone; it is in the past, but today, take a minute or two and observe the finer details surrounding this location.

Obviously, mirrors do play an important role in our lives. They can be found almost everywhere, in restaurants, hotels and airports. They are spotted and strategically placed in our vehicles, homes, churches or synagogues. They are popping up everywhere, even invading people's personal space or bubble.

Let's go ahead and put to test the winning formula under a full load. Let's discover and decide for ourselves if these five components really do hold up under pressure.

What's the main purpose or rationale behind glancing into a mirror in the first place? Well, to be quite honest with you, the main <u>Reasoning</u> for looking into any mirror is to simply check out and see how you look to yourself. So, while gazing straight ahead into the mirror, please pay close attention and notice all the unique and tiny details that may actually present themselves to you<u>. ...</u>
and here's why

Would you prefer if another person informed you that you had food stuck between your teeth, or would you rather discover it on your own by using a mirror? You may agree or disagree, but the real <u>Reason</u> behind looking into mirrors is to identify first and foremost what others may be subject to when they have to look at you. Case in point, would you rather discover a piece of food between your teeth by looking into a mirror or would you prefer another person telling you during an interview or meeting?

Let's move quickly towards the next component called Drawing concise Conclusions. Suppose while looking deeply into the mirror you noticed several long dark nose hairs protruding out of your left nostril? At this point in time, what's the right thing to do? That decision now sits squarely in the middle of your lap. Will you elect to groom those nose hairs or will you choose to let them protrude out?

As harsh as it may appear, this scenario requires some _Analytical Thinking_ on your part. Seriously, if you decide to leave the long nose hair protruding or hanging down, will your customers be less likely to buy your product? I do hope you would pause long enough to ponder the end-results. Have you calculated the financial impact of allowing a few nasty, unhealthy nose hairs to drive away customers?

Yes, Effort is at play here. It takes Effort to go stand directly in front of a mirror and look closely at your face. Potentially it could affect growth, sustainable revenue or increasing margins. Plus, it could also impact meaningful future relationships?

Yes, you are absolutely right. Legally, you have the free will to choose to let your nose hair protrude or hang down for the entire world to admire. Your rights are well protected, so grow your nose hair to any length that your heart desires. However, if by chance it makes your classmates, co-workers or customers nauseous to look at, would it be out of line for you to Pause long enough or Ponder the impact or end-results that your protruding nose hair just might have on others?

If your protruding nose hair causes a slight twinge of sickness or harm upon others, would it not be the proper, appropriate or the right thing to do, to just go ahead and neatly trim and groom them for their sakes? Should our Individual Rights or personal preferences be placed higher than those with whom we conduct business?

Maybe this is when and where "Professionalism" falls apart, when profits or our personal preferences are placed much higher than those around us. So, leading experts, should we ignore it, turn our backs and remain silent when decisions are made by those that directly or indirectly cause harm and discomfort on others?

Major Sporting Events: The Persona of Broadcasting   Perceived / Staged?

Bring up the lights, queue the microphones, three, two, one – action: camera's rolling on the set. Now that it's a live broadcast, take a closer look. Do you think all this professional persona is real, perceived or purposely staged for prime time viewers? Well to help answer that question, let's try this short and worthwhile exercise. It's pretty simple to complete. All you really need is an ink pen and some paper.

So, here's the game plan. Beginning today or tomorrow and running throughout the next four weeks, every time you get an opportunity to sit down to watch and enjoy a major sporting event that's being televised or broadcast, simply jot down a tiny check mark or the letter P on your piece of paper. Basically, what you are doing is keeping a running tally or scorecard at home. However for this particular experiment, I am not asking you to participate as if you were a loyal or casual sports fan, but rather, I am asking you to place a tiny check mark down, because you happen to be a responsible parent / guardian, community leader, consumer, registered voter or tax payer.

Once you have clearly recorded your presence, go ahead and start watching the entire telecast. If you could, try to catch the pre-game show too, paying particular attention to the <u>Persona</u> or professional image that's being projected. By that, I mean, notice the actual "Set" or staging area for the broadcasters and announcers to use. Begin to observe some of the finer details like the hair, makeup or apparel, such as the designer dresses, suits and ties being worn.

Up to this point, by all indications, it certainly appears that everything is first class, going smoothly and is a professional broadcast going as planned or scheduled. If you agree that this represents what you are truly observing or noticing, then go ahead and place a plus sign + next to your P or tiny check mark.

To complete this exercise, there's one final task remaining that I would like you to do. It's very important. Every time there's a commercial break or media time-out, instead of being in a hurry to flip through the other channels or head straight towards the refrigerator for a snack, I'd really like you to stay put for a moment and watch the entire series of ads or commercials. As you will later conclude, commercials and media time-outs play a significant role in the overall production of a major sporting event being televised.

Now remember, throughout the duration of the next four weeks, you are much more than just a typical sports fan. I am asking you to think as though you were a parent / guardian, community leader, consumer, registered voter or tax payer. As such, every time you observe an ad popping up during the media time-outs that displays rapid gun fire, people being blown up or bullets streaming across your screen I'd like for you to place a minus sign - next to all your other tiny marks.

Personal Scorecard/Your Running Tally

INSTRUCTIONS: Record your Presence with a letter P.
If you observe Professional Persona being projected then mark down a + sign.
Finally, during media time-outs, if you examine Promotional Ads depicting rapid gun-fire or people being blown up then simply mark down a - sign.

EXAMPLE: P = Presence   + = Persona   - = Promo

Football	Fighting Irish vs. Spartans	P + -
Basketball		
Racing	500	P + -
Baseball	Braves vs. Cubs	P + -
Soccer		
Golf		
Hockey		
Other		

At the end of Week Four, we will be adding up all the tiny marks you have placed on your personal scorecard. But more importantly, we need to remember that each of these tiny little - minus signs represent a victim or family member who is just trying to relax a little bit, perhaps take their minds off their loss and heartaches to enjoy a major sporting event. But because of all these 30- or 60-second commercials depicting rapid gun fire, people being blown and bullets streaming across their screen, their wounds are re-opened; the pain and agony of losing a loved one suddenly begins to resurface. It's like they never get a chance to really heal or work through the entire grieving process appropriately.

If you will, take a good long look at the following numbers. In fact, to absorb or feel the full magnitude of these staggering figures, try reciting them out loud.

"U.S. Military Casualties"[1]

1993	Vietnam	58,148 killed Average Age 23 years old
1950	Korean War	36,516 killed, 92,134 wounded
1918	World War I	116,516 killed
1945	World War II	295,000 killed

"School Shootings"2

Oct 2, 2006	Lancaster County, PA	5 Amish girls killed, 5 wounded
Apr 17, 2007	Virginia Tech Massacre	33 killed, 15 wounded
Oct 10, 2007	Success Tech Academy	1 killed, 4 shot
Apr 20, 1999	Columbine High School	15 killed, 21 injured

29

Nov 7, 2006	University of Miami	1 Football Player killed
Sep 21, 2011	Morningside heights	1 H.S. Basketball Player killed
Feb 6, 2011	Near Youngstown State	1 killed, 11 suffered wounds
Dec 14, 2012	Sandy Hook Elementary	26 killed

"Leadership"3

Jan 9, 2011	Rep. Gabrielle Giffords	18 shot upon, 6 killed
1981	President Reagan	1 Shot
1963	President John F. Kennedy	1 killed
1968	Bobby Kennedy	1 killed
Apr 4, 1968	Martin Luther King	1 killed
Apr 14,1865	President Lincoln	1 killed

"Public Places"4

Dec 5, 2007	Westroads Mall Omaha, NE	9 killed 4 wounded
Nov 28, 2008	Toys "R" Us Palm Desert, CA	2 killed
July 20, 2012	Aurora, CO Theater	12 killed 58 injured

Upon catching your breath, now try imagining how the surviving victims, siblings or families from Sandy Hook Elementary, Columbine High School and Virginia Tech must feel or what they experience, when they sit down to relax and watch a major sporting event. Then completely out of the blue, without warning - the dreadful reminders of their tragic loss appear across their screen.

There are times when I find myself thinking about our military families or even the next of kin of those who have been innocently gunned down in our crowded shopping malls or neighborhood streets.

According to the American Association of Psychology, children will watch 8,000 murders before they turn age 12.[5] Research also indicates that children in the United States watch 4 hours of Television per day.[6] This correlates to children being exposed to over 20,000 commercials a year; that's about 55 per day. Research also shows that by the time an average child enters elementary school he will have seen 100,000 acts of violence on TV.

I get it. I fully understand the merit behind why "Market Research Studies" are so valuable. And yes, I know all about obtaining pertinent data so strategies can be set up to target those distinct segments. But I am also smart enough to know that real numbers don't lie and that believe it or not, there are two sides to every equation. In other words, if your research indicates that X number of people are "demanding" this type of drama, people being blown up and rapid gun fire, then there's a group or Y number of people preferring that you not ignore their time to heal. There are plenty of other time slots to show and promote all the deadly drama and suspense, but out of respect, not during major sporting events.

Mentally start thinking about the "Effort" that the Networks put into all these telecasts. And even though it may not be your cup of tea, do some calculating or "Analytical Thinking" on exactly how much revenue is generated from producing this major sporting event. Consider the "Reasoning" or motivation behind these commercials. Are you "Drawing concise Conclusions" on the content and subject matter?

"Making wise Intelligent Decisions." Let's be certain that we are considering and reviewing all the numbers. In this particular situation, it's imperative that we not only understand, but also be willing to respect the entire "Market." For example, if one out of seven Americans will lose a parent or sibling before the age of 20, then perhaps the proper thing to do is not to air those promotional ads depicting rapid gun fire or people being blown up during major sporting events, especially if our Core Values and Mission Statements clearly support such initiatives.

Compiled below are a few core values and mission statements. Again, do not rush or try to skim over these commitments. See if you can pick out or determine who they will be targeting or perhaps what services or product they hope to provide.

Allstate Mission Statement: "*To be the best…serving our customers by providing peace of mind and enriching their quality of life through our partnership in the management of the risks they face.*"[7]

State Farm Insurance:

Mission is to help people manage the risk of everyday life, recover from the unexpected, and realize their dreams.[8]

Chick-Fil-A Mission Statement: "Be America's Best Quick-Service Restaurant"

Chick-Fil-A are national sponsors of Core Essentials, a value education curriculum designed around three ideas: Treat Others Right, Make Smart Decisions and Maximize Your Potential.[9]

The NASCAR Foundation:

The NASCAR Foundation is dedicated to helping children learn how to win, both inside and outside the classroom, through a variety of educational opportunities. The NASCAR Foundation embodies the compassion of the NASCAR Family and its commitment to serving communities. The NASCAR Foundation seeks to raise funds and increase volunteerism to support nonprofit charities and charitable causes throughout the nation with an emphasis on initiatives that affect the ability of children to live, learn and play.[10]

LOWES: "We will provide customer-valued solutions with the best prices, products and services to make Lowe's the first choice for home improvement." In order to make their vision a reality Lowe's focuses its employees on these values. Customer Focused, Teamwork, Ownership, Passion For Execution, Respect and Integrity.[11]

THE NCAA "Is to govern competition in a fair, safe, equitable and sportsmanlike manner, and to integrate intercollegiate athletics into higher education so that the educational experience of the student-athlete is paramount."

The NCAA works with some of America's top corporations to help promote the value of athletics in education. The companies provide funding and expertise to support youth programs, fan interactive experiences and scholarship programs for student-athletes, in addition to promoting the excitement of the NCAA's championships.[12]

SOUTHEASTERN CONFERENCE: "The purpose of the Southeastern Conference is to assist its member institutions in the maintenance of programs of intercollegiate athletics which are compatible with the highest standards of education and competitive sports."[13]

BOYS & GIRLS CLUB OF AMERICA: "To enable all young people, especially those who need us most, to reach their full potential as productive, caring, responsible citizens." Core Beliefs: A Boys & Girls Club Provides

A safe place to learn and grow . . . Ongoing relationships with caring, adult professionals . . .

Life-enhancing programs and character development experiences . . . Hope and opportunity.[14]

THE FIRST TEE: Campaign for reaching 10 million Young People

To impact the lives of young people by providing educational programs that build character, instill life-enhancing values and promote healthy choices through the game of golf.

Our Nine Values, Honesty, Integrity, Sportsmanship, Respect, Confidence, Responsibility, Perseverance, Courtesy and Judgment.[15]

JOSEPH INSTITUTE: To improve the ethical quality of society by changing personal and organizational decision making and behavior.[16]

GIRLSCOUTS MISSION: Girl Scouting builds girls of courage, confidence, and character, who make the world a better place.[17]

GRAMMY AWARDS: "The Recording Academy" "To positively impact the lives of musicians, industry members and our society at large."[18]

EMMY AWARDS: "The mission of the Academy is to promote creativity, diversity, innovation and excellence through recognition, education and leadership in the advancement of the telecommunications and sciences."[19]

BEN DAVIS HIGH SCHOOL: Athletic Event Expectations

Be respectful of game officials, players, coaches, opposing fans, and facilities.

Cheer positively during the introduction of players, coaches, and officials.

Cheer positively for their team and to refrain from negative cheering and chants directed toward their opponents.

Demonstrate a concern for injured players on either team.

Remember that they represent not only their school, but their community and family as well.

Conduct themselves in an appropriate and civil manner.

Be respectful of game officials, players, coaches, opposing fans, and facilities.

Cheer positively during the introduction of players, coaches, and officials.

Cheer positively for their team and to refrain from negative cheering and chants directed toward their opponents.

Demonstrate a concern for injured players on either team.

Remember that they represent not only their school, but their community and family as well.

Conduct themselves in an appropriate and civil manner.

Parents and Fans are expected to:

Respect game officials, players, coaches, and fans.

Recognize outstanding performances on either side of the playing field.

Be exemplary role models of sportsmanship by supporting teams in every positive manner possible, including content of cheers

and signs.

Maintain composure at all times.

Student Athletes are expected to:

Be respectful of teammates and opponents before, during, and after each contest.

Be gracious in victory or defeat.

Play within the rules and accept the outcomes, win or lose.

Conduct themselves at all times with honesty, integrity, poise, and composure.

Be respectful of the officials.

Demonstrate sportsmanship at all times and act as positive role models.

Coaches are expected to:

Set, promote, maintain standards of good sportsmanship with their coaching staffs, students, athletes, and fans.

Respect decisions of game officials and behave appropriately in their interactions with officials.

Maintain their composure at all times.

Use positive coaching techniques to motivate and teach desired results.

Treat mistakes as opportunities for learning.

Positively acknowledge the efforts of their opponents.[20]

HOMEWOOD HIGH SCHOOL MARCHING BAND: Professionalism, Pride, Perfection[21]

NFL Play 60: "To make the next generation of youth the most active and healthy"[22]

Papa John's Pizza: Papa John's will create superior brand loyalty, i.e. "raving fans", through a authentic, superior-quality products, b legendary customer service and c exceptional community service.[23]

University of Georgia: "The University System of Georgia will create a more educated Georgia, well prepared for a global, technological society, by providing first-rate undergraduate and graduate education, leading-edge research, and committed public service." The mission of the University System of Georgia is to contribute to the educational, cultural, economic, and social advancement of Georgia by providing excellent undergraduate general education and first-rate programs leading to associate, baccalaureate, masters, professional, and doctorate degrees; by pursuing leading-edge basic and applied research, scholarly inquiry, and creative endeavors; and by bringing these intellectual resources, and those of the public libraries, to bear on the economic development of the State and the continuing education of its citizens.

The mission of the Chancellor's Office is to serve the University System of Georgia, its Board of Regents and thirty-five institutions, the State of Georgia, and other constituencies by providing leadership in higher education and stewardship of state and University System resources.

- The Chancellor's Office will promote a statewide perspective on higher education that attends to the current and developing needs of the State, its citizens and students, and relates them effectively to the University System and its institutions.

- The Chancellor's Office will support the Board of Regents in furthering and achieving its vision for the University System by providing leadership in analyzing, monitoring, and anticipating higher education trends and developments, and by planning strategically for the future of the University System. [24]

Norte Dame University: The University seeks to cultivate in its students not only an appreciation for the great achievements of human beings, but also a disciplined sensibility to the poverty, injustice, and oppression that burden the lives of so many. The aim is to create a sense of human solidarity and concern for the common good that will bear fruit as learning becomes service to justice.

The University of Notre Dame is a Catholic academic community of higher learning, animated from its origins by the Congregation of Holy Cross. The University is dedicated to the pursuit and sharing of truth for its own sake. As a Catholic university, one of its distinctive goals is to provide a forum where, through free inquiry and open discussion, the various lines of Catholic thought may intersect with all the forms of knowledge found in the arts, sciences, professions, and every other area of human scholarship and creativity.

The intellectual interchange essential to a university requires, and is enriched by, the presence and voices of diverse scholars and students. The Catholic identity of the University depends upon, and is nurtured by, the continuing presence of a predominant number of Catholic intellectuals. This ideal has been consistently maintained by the University leadership throughout its history. What the University asks of all its scholars and students, however, is not a particular creedal affiliation, but a respect for the objectives of Notre

Dame and a willingness to enter into the conversation that gives it life and character. Therefore, the University insists upon academic freedom that makes open discussion and inquiry possible.

The University prides itself on being an environment of teaching and learning that fosters the development in its students of those disciplined habits of mind, body, and spirit that characterize educated, skilled, and free human beings. In addition, the University seeks to cultivate in its students not only an appreciation for the great achievements of human beings but also a disciplined sensibility to the poverty, injustice and oppression that burden the lives of so many. The aim is to create a sense of human solidarity and concern for the common good that will bear fruit as learning becomes service to justice.

Notre Dame also has a responsibility to advance knowledge in a search for truth through original inquiry and publication. This responsibility engages the faculty and students in all areas of the University, but particularly in graduate and professional education and research. The University is committed to constructive and critical engagement with the whole of human culture.

The University encourages a way of living consonant with a Christian community and manifest in prayer, liturgy and service. Residential life endeavors to develop that sense of community and of responsibility that prepares students for subsequent leadership in building a society that is at once more human and more divine.

Notre Dame's character as a Catholic academic community presupposes that no genuine search for the truth in the human or the cosmic order is alien to the life of faith. The University welcomes all areas of scholarly activity as consonant with its mission, subject to appropriate critical refinement. There is, however, a special obligation and opportunity, specifically as a Catholic university, to pursue the religious dimensions of all human learning. Only thus can Catholic intellectual life in all disciplines be animated and fostered and a proper community of scholarly religious discourse be established.

In all dimensions of the University, Notre Dame pursues its objectives through the formation of an authentic human community graced by the Spirit of Christ[25]

Virginia Commonwealth University: Code of Ethics Virginia Commonwealth University id committed to an environment of uncompromising integrity and ethic conduct. Our ethical standards are the foundation for our decisions and actions. As members of the faculty, staff and administration of VCU your actions will be guided by these principles and values: Respect: We will respect individuals, diversity and the rights of others. Honesty: We will act and communicate honestly and candidly. We will not mislead others. Excellence: We will strive for excellence in all we that we do. Responsibility and accountability. We will be responsible and accountable for our decisions and actions.

Stewardship: We will be good stewards of the resources entrusted to the university. Compliance: We will understand and comply with the codes, laws, regulations, policies and procedures that govern our university activities. Virginia Commonwealth University's strategic plan, Quest for Distinction, rest upon four themes that outline the university's institutional priorities, strategies and initiatives.

Theme I. Become a leader among national research universities in providing all students with high quality learning/living experiences focused on inquiry, discovery and innovation in a global environment.

Theme II. Attain preeminence as an urban, public research university by making contributions in research, scholarship, creative expression and clinical practice that bring national and international recognition.

Theme III. Achieve national recognition as a fully-integrated research university with a commitment to human health.

Theme IV. Become a national model for community engagement and regional impact.[26]

Obviously this list could go on and on. Nonetheless, it's a pretty good cross section of our beliefs and visions. So now the question remains, will we stand firm behind these words or commitments?

When the milk in your refrigerator turns repulsive and sour, you have no problem turning your nose from that stench. You are quick to toss it out.

In contrast we see no reaction, no "EFFORT" in preventing victims and their family members from getting ill over the sour ads being aired during major sporting events and having their wounds reopened.

The thought and mindset of, "It's not my job, not my call or decision to make" is no different than leaving that sour milk container for the next person to deal with.

It's astounding that one moment you are enthralled by watching Arnold Palmer informing us about the lasting benefits of golf among youngsters and how the First Tee Program is striving to reach a million kids, then within a blink of an eye, we are shifted to viewing people being killed and blown up. Is that the vision or mission we are aiming for? Do we want our mission statement to be as good as our word?

"You Have My "<u>WORD</u>" On It"

"Well, that is, unless of course, no one is actually really watching me. Then it's sort of up in the air, whether I'll do the right thing or not, you know, just depends."   Wink-Wink / Pinkie Promise

Okay, is that a valiant attempt at some tongue-in-cheek humor, or is that pretty much how the new normal tends to roll?

What's your take on that interesting sign hanging up in the public restrooms of your favorite eating establishments, posted by the owner and local health department asking that <u>all</u> associates wash their hands prior to returning to their work stations – Now, does that request mean 100% of the time or is 65% of the time acceptable? As a frequent patron, what's your take? Are you hoping and expecting 100% participation, or are you willing to accept it if only 65% of the staff wash their hands prior to handling your meal?

I think we have all grown up a tad bit and have learned a valuable lesson from the devastating Penn State coaching scandal — and that is, knowing more and not doing more is inexcusable.

Recently, the NCAA handed down some strict sanctions regarding this somber situation. Although what's more impressive, is that they didn't shy away from expressing or announcing an interest in <u>driving cultural change</u>.

Well then, let's make that happen. We have before us a golden opportunity to actually do more because we know more.

I'd like to suggest that we try this: Whereas University Presidents, Athletic Directors, Conference Commissioners and Corporate Partners begin having healthy discussions and negotiations with the appropriate Networks towards implementing and steering this culture change.

If discussions and decisions can occur for realigning super or power conferences, then surely we can have some serious dialogue concerning people being harmed or killed during media time-outs.

If discussions and decisions can occur for negotiating multi-million dollar television contracts, then surely, we can have some serious dialogue concerning bullets streaming across our screens during media time-outs.

If discussions and decisions can occur for selecting the most deserving and competitive teams for a popular March Madness tournament, then surely we can have some serious dialogue concerning rapid gun fire during media time-outs.

So, yes driving culture change, as the NCAA has suggested, is possible. It's just a matter of getting the right people together who are willing to do the right thing.

Just look at what Major League Baseball has been able to accomplish. Through open and honest discussions, they were able to come together, communicate and reach a favorable decision on how they were going to pay tribute to Jackie Robinson, a special Hall of Famer.

Seriously, we should all be tipping our caps to this kind of solid leadership. Notice they didn't buckle under or back down from their commitments by saying, "well, if we can get at least 65% of our teams to participate, then surely that would be a success."

No, MLB took a stance and kept true to their words, by engaging 100% participation, meaning that on April 15th, every team, every player; including all the on-field personnel will be wearing the same jersey number 42 out of respect for Hall of Famer, Jackie Robinson.

So, you see, healthy discussions, proper negotiations and solid decisions can produce results as well as creating positive change.

Unfortunately, we still have to be subject to all the ridicule along the way. In fact, I wish I had a dollar for every time I heard this exact slur or remark; "Dude, it's only entertainment, so get over it." In other words, "entertainment" by its own omission deserves a free pass; in spite of being callous or uncaring about their audience. It's as if they are trying to convince us that "entertainment" is infallible and can do no wrong.

The notion that somehow our youngsters can mentally separate or distinguish real-life-emotions from that of pure entertainment is simply rubbish and irresponsible.

The National Basketball Association understands this. And yes, even though the high flying, wide eyed entertainment world has weaved itself into the forefront of Professional Basketball, the NBA governing body still felt compelled enough to invoke their Anti-Flopping (faking a foul) policy in order to protect the overall integrity of the game.

The USA Football National Governing Body has raised the bar even higher. Not only are they concerned with helmet-to-helmet injuries and concussions, but they have committed themselves to teaching and training proper fundamentals. What I admire most is their willingness to reach out to all parties concerned, including coaches, officials, parents and kids just starting out. Keep in mind, this is not just for the benefit of current players; but for the most part it's done out of respect for the former players and their family members who themselves have witnessed a horrific injury or experienced the impact of death.[27]

If we are going to get serious about driving culture change, then we better step up our game and bring "Professionalism" to the forefront. No more playing around, No lame excuses and definitely no more lip service. Obviously, the prime time rhetoric or verbal mudslinging isn't accomplishing squat.

We can't afford to keep doing the same ole – same ole and expect to experience or see new results. Perhaps, now is the time we roll up our sleeves and try something totally different. With that being said; I'd like to suggest that for the next two years, we not only embrace "Professionalism" and it's sturdy structure, but that each of us will actually live out and model true "Professionalism" in all facets of our lives. From the very moment we lift up our heads off our pillow until the time we lay it back down again, "Professionalism" should permeate then naturally radiate from among us.

Sure it's going to be a tad awkward and weird. Sure it's going to require some new and exciting approaches, but you know what? Once we start to observe the benefits and see the positive end-results, it will be totally worth all the effort.

You see what happens is that throughout the course of a routine day we fall prey to this thing that traditionally some may call the human rat race; however, that's putting it mildly. It's more like being drawn into this raging, out-of-control, chaotic cesspool of smelly rotten senseless busywork. Fill this form out, clear the paper jam, complete or work on that report; be sure to check all the boxes that apply. When you have finished, log on, scroll down, tap on the drop down box, then click the link, be sure to save and submit.

Routinely, we spend a lot of energy chasing after our own tail with redundancy. If that alone is not enough for us to scream or pull our hair out, then just wait a second, because there's more. Compound all this massive confusion with being instructed to push one for that department or push two to reach another division, be sure to push the pound sign to hear all the remaining options. Please hold.

Whether you are applying for a home mortgage, student loan, pulling a building permit, or simply trying to resolve a medical claim that's been denied, the number of hoops and hurdles that you must climb over is just astronomical and absurd. Before you know it, you have quickly become annoyed, agitated and irritable. It's awfully difficult to practice or demonstrate "Professionalism" when you are knee deep and sinking in pure frustration.

Typically, your day is already full of major requirements and tight time restraints, so the last thing you need is another form or report being added to your plate. Instead of focusing on providing or offering "Professionalism" we get side tracked and start displaying a rash of rudeness.

If you are not careful or mindful, all this red tape can easily tie you up in tiny knots, to the point where "Professionalism" has been completely choked out of your demeanor or personality. Losing that zeal or zest is both physically and mentally draining. So that's precisely why we need to start working together towards changing and pruning the landscape of "Professionalism."

While the University Presidents, Conference Commissioners, Athletic Directors, Corporate Sponsors along with the NCAA are negotiating their strategies for culture change with the major Networks, remember there are plenty of other opportunities for you and me to get involved.

Over the next two years, Civic and Chamber members can work closely with small business owners and local vendors to raise "Professionalism" to a higher level of importance. Also, School Officials and Teachers can begin implementing "Professionalism" within their daily lesson plans.

Over the next twenty-four months, Board members can start to review and report back on how they are tracking or measuring Professionalism Effort, Analytical Thinking, Reasoning, Drawing concise Conclusions and Making wise Intelligent Decisions.

This will open up the lines of communication for staff and supervisors to eliminate the barriers that are causing the greatest stress, so "Professionalism" can once again flourish instead of just floundering, hurting morale and reducing profit margins.

Over the next 730 days, "Professionalism" could certainly serve as a vital tool as we strive to build stronger diplomatic and global allies. So you see, no one is exempt. It's going to take a cohesive and collaborative effort from everyone to bring "Professionalism" front and center. However:

If we choose to do nothing, then the lack of "Professionalism" will continue to chase away and run off paying customers.

If we choose to do nothing, then the lack of "Professionalism" will continue to create disgruntled employees and associates.

If we choose to do nothing, then the lack of "Professionalism" will continue to deteriorate and destroy our core values.

So here's the bottom line. Consider the risk of doing nothing compared to the rewards and dividends of collectively raising "Professionalism" to the next level. The benefit and true beauty behind all of this is knowing that "Professionalism" is a constant derivative of "People Skills." In other words, if we teach and develop "Professionalism" then proportionately we will see sustainable and steady growth in how our "People Skills" are demonstrated, delivered and displayed.

I mean, my goodness, if we can find the time to celebrate and recognize National Pecan Month or National Chocolate Lover Month[29] then surely we ought to be able to find the time and energy to advocate for and promote "Professionalism."

We know more so let's do more!

II

<u>*PEOPLE SKILLS*</u>
Cleverly Disguised/Distorted

Picture this: You're walking down the corridor of an extremely busy, overly crowded terminal when suddenly, a loud overhead announcement catches your attention; "Paging, I Really Can't Be Bothered – Paging, I Really Can't Be Bothered."

Wow, wouldn't that be a shock or jolt? Just mentioning such an occurrence seems a bit odd and absurd. Well then, what about this scenario: you find yourself stepping out of an elevator of a prominent teaching hospital to hear these echoing words; "Paging, I Really Don't Care – Paging, I Really Don't Care." Once again, very strange and quite surprising to say the least.

But you know what, if you earnestly look around and listen to how we truly speak or treat one another, in actuality, the above PAGES are not that difficult to fathom. Sure those exact words may not be expressed or stated verbatim, but certainly their undertones, subtleties and innuendos are felt and heard just as loud and clear. In fact, just as piercing too.

Sometime during the next few days, go ask at least five different individuals—perhaps your neighbors, friends, co-workers or classmates—to rate their overall "People Skills." Seriously, don't be shy; ask them straight up to rate how they perceive their "People Skills." If need be, rely on the old traditional or standard scale of one to ten, with ten being great and one indicating poor skills. Ask them to provide you with their honest take on how they would best describe or identify their "People Skills."

Listen intently, observing how these individuals not only formulate but present their answers. Without any real hesitation, the majority of responses you will likely encounter will sound something similar to this; "Oh, you mean my 'People Skills.' Why of course, they are wonderful." or "You've got to be kidding me, my 'People Skills' are fantastic. Matter of fact, they're excellent."

Invariably these comments are quickly followed by a barrage of personal pleas or pats on the back, sounding like this; "No really, I am very polite and considerate" or "I am always friendly and courteous." Not once, have I ever heard anyone say; "Gee you know what, you're right, my "People Skills" are absolutely horrific, they're awful, in fact they're just plain pitiful."

Up to this point it certainly does appear as though everyone is scoring themselves on the high end or taking the stance that their "People Skills" are above average or exceptional. But, let's move that measuring needle around for a brief moment and put it smack dab, squarely on our own set of "People Skills." Surely the end-results will be the same, correct?

Sometime today on a separate piece of paper, jot down the names of the last three or four individuals you carried on a complete or solid conversation with before calling it quits for the day. Preferably, this should be an actual dialogue you held in person, although with technology being as prevalent and accessible as it is, certainly you may include any pertinent conversations you had while using your electronic device. However, the main focus here is that you pause for a moment and physically write out the first and last names of all the individuals you most recently had a direct discussion with. Knowing the first and last name is a test in and of itself, isn't it?

Then if you will, carefully think back upon these verbal exchanges. Okay, being completely honest, were these conversations productive and meaningful? Were you respectful, considerate or somewhat condescending? Do you recall whether you were polite a pompous ass, or somewhere in between?

Notice throughout the first part of this assignment, just how easy it was for everyone to rattle off and admit to having wonderful or great "People Skills" but then based upon the situation or severity of their direct conversations, suddenly those well-thought-of "People Skills" became a bit more challenging to execute. In fact, more times than not our first instinct is to simply put all these high-powered, fancy "People Skills" on hold so we can rip someone a new one in the grocery store, at the post office, at a sporting event, in church, at school, in traffic, on social media, any and everywhere.

Unfortunately, the mindset of our pop culture is that it's perfectly acceptable to compromise or place "People Skills" on temporary administrative leave, so they can puff up and bite someone's head off. This type of attitude is not acceptable on any level and must be reversed**. ... and here's why**

<u>MANNERS</u>: After Age Eleven Insignificant / Non-Applicable N/A

Push in your chair, cover your mouth when you cough, respect your elders, pick up after yourself, express courtesy by saying, "Please" and gratitude by saying, "Thank You."

Wow, am I miss something here? Since when did all these acts of kindness or manners become optional? I mean come on now; who authorized such a thing to happen? Do you recall an executive order or formal proclamation stating that kind gestures or manners are no longer necessary after age eleven?

Somehow, somewhere along the way, we have allowed manners and the role they play in our lives to be completely knocked off kilter. It's like they've become totally obsolete and insignificant. What's worse, is that kind gestures are being kicked to the curb where everyone is just nonchalantly stepping over them as though they never existed. As far as I am concerned, this is totally unacceptable and needs to be fixed, immediately. **. . . and here's why**

One doesn't have to be smarter than a first grader to figure out that if you lack manners, you lack "People Skills" which tragically means you lack

"Professionalism." But wait just one dog gone minute; what if we collectively agreed to reverse this negative trend by reinstating manners into our society? We know more, so let's do more. Why suffer the risk of doing nothing?

Resurgence 180: Turning Things Around

I'd like to suggest that every ninth grader in our high schools, whether they are in the public or private sector, or being home schooled spend 50 hours volunteering at the local Health Department. The education observed and the firsthand experience of assisting the walk-in recipients would benefit everyone involved. More than likely, this type of real life-training would serve as a valuable eye-opening or "ah-ha" moment. At the completion of their 50 hours, students would be guided through a culminating activity involving the economics and accounting principles of how our current welfare system works, to include a 500-word essay.

I also think that every Tenth Grader, again in either a public, private or home school should spend 50 hours volunteering at a local Detox center. Upon the completion of their volunteer hours of mopping floors, cleaning restrooms or making up cots, students should engage in an intense follow up presentation addressing drug and alcohol abuse as well as death and dying.

Based upon my thirty plus years of officiating high school basketball, I definitely see where this age group could benefit the most by writing a simple 1,000 word essay involving pertinent components and personal accomplishments found in most obituaries.

Okay, now stay with me. I would also like to see every Eleventh Grader spend 50 hours volunteering at a local jail or correctional facility and journaling their experiences. This will segue to formal discussions regarding choices and consequences.

Finally, as Twelfth Graders, the combined experiences over the course of their academic careers would allow them to generate a 2,000-word essay including three solid examples of how these activities and experiences impacted their understanding and application of the Golden Rule.

If you think for one moment that implementing Resurgence 180 is pure rubbish or you think that I am totally way off-base, then do me a favor. Over the next few days stop by your local shopping mall, hang out near the food court for a while, and observe the general public passing by. Then ask yourself, as strong Business Leaders, Guardians or School Administrators have we done everything within our means to ignite a thirst or hunger for knowledge? Perhaps Resurgence 180 could be that extra spark to revive professionalism. Just think, at the end of four years, our future leaders would have already logged over 200 hours of first-hand, front-line experience. Definitely worth pursuing.

Our Personality Traits   Moody / Temperamental
<u>Never Realized</u>

While I was attending college, I was dealt the luxury of a four-and-half-hour layover at the O'Hara International Airport in Chicago. At first, I thought to myself, this is not going to be good. Time, I am sure, will just drag on and on, but as I sat there and started to People Watch the hours actually flew by. Not only was I mesmerized by my surroundings, but I was also fascinated with the different types of characters and personalities hustling all about and heading off in various directions.

I suppose that's why to this day, I have the utmost respect for Carl G. Jung, a Swiss psychiatrist, along with Katherine Cook Briggs and her daughter Isabel Briggs Meyers for spending endless hours analyzing people's personalities and behaviors.[28]

Their distinct research is unique and has proven time after time to be quite useful. Especially, and I am paraphrasing here, when determining which of the 16 measuring pods individuals gravitate towards. In other words, let's say you were given the task of hand-picking twelve individuals to serve on a challenging group project. Based upon our knowledge that people have different strengths and weaknesses, it wouldn't be prudent or beneficial for you to select only "Oranges." Certainly you would want to pick a few, apples, plums or pears to help round out your winning team.

Whether you represent Management or Labor, "People Skills" are equally shared. Everyone must practice "People Skills." No one is exempt. Although we come together in different shapes and sizes, technically we score either as an extravert or introvert, shy or outgoing, but the bottom line is we must comply and practice great "People Skills."

Never Noticed: My Sleeping Pillow   How Valuable / Until It Was Tossed Aside

Tonight, of all nights, go about your normal and typical bedtime routine, locking the doors, checking your alarm clock and turning off the lights. Then crawl into bed, pull those sheets up nice and snug to you, but then just prior to laying your head down, reach up and remove your sleeping pillow. Seriously, reach up and gently place that pillow down towards the bottom of your bed. Okay, begin lying back down, with only your head resting on the mattress.

Were you comfortable or did you start to experience some difficulty falling asleep without the use of a pillow supporting your head? The term sleeping pillow is synonymous with obtaining a good night's sleep, just as the term "People Skills" is synonymous with achieving "Professionalism."

Sure, it's possible to fall asleep without the aid of a pillow, but why would you put yourself in that kind of predicament? So tell me, is this something you feel you can manage night after night, or would you prefer having your firm / fluffy sleeping pillow back?

Are You A Subpar Napkin Or A Warm Wash Cloth? Profound Difference:

One cold, chilly afternoon in rural Indiana, while I was a senior in High School, my mother politely asked me if I would stop by the skilled nursing home and visit my great aunt who had recently suffered a CVA stroke. At first, I thought to myself, sure thing, no problem. I knew this request would not be that difficult to accomplish, especially knowing that this particular skilled nursing home she was talking about was only a few blocks from my High School. So I thought to myself, piece of cake, I can handle this simple chore.

But then came this very long pause in her voice. My mom proceeded to add several caveats to her original request. She said; "Jon Marc, while you are standing there in your great Aunt's room, I would like for you to go over to her bed-side stand, open the drawer, reach in and grab that tiny bottle of your Aunt's favorite perfume." She continued by saying; "I want you to gently lean down and spray a tiny hint of that perfume and fragrance on her pillow case, because your great Aunt was a proud and proper woman, and even though she is lying there unable to speak or move any parts of her body, she would want to smell nice, so I am asking that you to do this kind gesture for her sake." Well as you can imagine, I did not disappoint my mom. I followed her exact instructions. More importantly, that day, I discovered the profound difference between being just a "Napkin" compared to being a "Warm Wash Cloth."

You see as a "Napkin" you simply honor the first part of the obligation by making a quick, short visit to the nursing home, but as a "Warm Wash Cloth" not only do you honor the first part of that request, but you engage yourself in doing an extra kind gesture like reaching down, grabbing that tiny bottle of perfume and spraying a tiny mist of fragrance on the pillow case of a motionless patient who would want to smell nice for her visiting friends and neighbors. That's what you call being a "Warm Wash Cloth."

Customer Service represents being a napkin; whereas, Customer Satisfaction represents being a Warm Wash Cloth.

Notice being a Napkin or Warm Wash Cloth has nothing to do with how much money you make or title you hold, but simply your willingness to serve others thoroughly.

I don't believe for one minute that my mom was nagging, preaching or even trying to prejudge my actions, but clearly wanted to ensure or clarify that I fully understood the purpose of my visit. More importantly, she wanted to ensure that I fully grasped the much larger purpose behind the meaning of life, which is being concerned for others.

Seriously, if you are not a bit interested in what others may be feeling, thinking or possibly needing, then you might as well put this book down. Because great "People Skills" requires a deeper understanding of how we communicate and how we treat others morning, noon and night.

To me it's mind boggling that Labor Costs and the expenses surrounding labor appears on our monthly financial statements, yet Customer Satisfaction is left completely off, nowhere to be found.

You would think that if your staff fully understood the profound difference between being a Warm Wash Cloth compared to that of being just another Subpar Napkin that prosperity and the end-results created from those actions would have your revenues growing off the charts.

We spend a great deal of time asking technical questions on our annual performance improvement evaluations. For example, have you completed the Sexual Harassment or Corporate Compliance training? – check. How's your attendance? – check. How's your documentation; is it timely, an accurate? – check.

Why not come out and ask the more pertinent or practical questions. For example; how many times did you roll your eyes in front of our customers or co-workers this past year? Did you grumble or mumble under your breath where paying customers or co-workers could hear you?

Measuring whether someone's performance truly Exceeds, Meets or Needs Improvement depends upon the types of questions being asked. More importantly, tracking productivity depends upon whether someone is either a Subpar Napkin or a Warm Wash Cloth. Looking at your organization right now, how many Subpar Napkins do you have compared to Warm Wash Cloths?

Are you one of the napkins?

III

<u>*PRIORITIES*</u> *Scornfully*
Under-Utilized/Gone Amiss

Eat . . . Sleep . . . and make Beaucoup (Boo Coo) Bucks - Need I say more?

Everyone in their rightful place and mind knows that eating, sleeping and making lots of money are the only sensible "priorities" worth pursuing. Hands down, end of story.

Before you start celebrating, dancing a jig or shouting from the roof tops, "I Told You So" - "I Told You So" could you at least do me one last favor and re-read the title of this book. In fact, read it out loud . . . nice and slow.

Perhaps <u>YES</u> terday, while still naïve and quite impressionable in my abilities and overall thinking, I might have fallen for such shallow or simplistic advice, but definitely <u>NO</u> t today**. . . . and here's why**

You see, the word scornfully is vital to our growth and understanding. It means intentionally dismissing, rejecting or having very little regard for people, places or things. Now take the word priorities which literally can be described as a complete listing of tasks or a preferential order - relative to their importance. So, the direct result of connecting scornfully with priorities is that finally we have some solid and concrete answers to work with.

Linking together scornfully and priorities explains fully why we are in this global mess . . . in the first place.

We now can pin point and know with absolute certainty why we are experiencing so much craziness happening all around us. Seriously, it's not that difficult to track with accuracy where the quantifying outliers are occurring. It's so blatant and obvious - but when Humans from top to bottom, intentionally dismiss, reject or willfully kick pressing matters of importance to the curb, then it's a no brainer, why we are seeing so much upheaval and chaotic behavior creep in and prevail over our daily lives.

Why . . . It's All Making Sense . . . Now: Small Procedures make a Big Difference.

Lower . . . That Landing . . . Gear . . . Pilots / Passengers

Traveling to your favorite destination can be fun and exhilarating, especially when your itinerary is jam - packed with adventures and planned activities. Plus, isn't it nice to physically and mentally get away, able to shred your busy, hectic schedule and start relaxing a bit?

So, as a passenger sitting on that plane, slowly descending from the sky, anticipating a much needed arrival, is lowering the landing gear a high or low priority for you?

It depends on the context of the question, right? Well, you would certainly hope that for the trained pilots monitoring the instruments, maneuvering the flaps and props, lowering the landing gear at the appropriate altitude would definitely be considered a top priority.

It's absolutely astounding when you count up the number of Human lives affected directly or indirectly by this one aviation procedure. Stop and think about just how far these branches reach, from the manufacturing engineers, to the service mechanics, to the families and friends waiting at the terminal. We are talking millions.

So perhaps following proper "Procedures" is worth pursuing.

Blood Work . . . Needle Sticks . . . X 3 . . . Phlebotomist / Patient

Clinically, I get it. I fully understand that lab work can greatly assist the Primary Care Physician in detecting or preventing diseases early. Perhaps that's why I didn't flinch, when asked to have my current blood count and sugar levels tested or screened.

I certainly would like to know if my lab results are within or outside the normal range, but being pricked three times was definitely not on my to do list, and I can't imagine it was a high priority for the phlebotomist. Usually, the protocol is that your appointment is scheduled and you're instructed to FAST for twelve hours prior to having your blood drawn. This means, you are allowed no food - no drinks.

My "priorities" that particular morning were to arrive bright and early, be gently stuck by a tiny little needle and then be sent on my merry way. Unfortunately that didn't occur. The Phlebotomist had a very difficult time trying to find a healthy vain. Finally after two needle sticks to my arm, a clinical supervisor standing nearby turned towards me and simply asked, "Have you had any water this morning?" I stated, "No, I was told to FAST no food or drinks."

The clinician calmly grabbed my shoulder, gave me a smile and said, "Next time you have blood work, drink some water; consuming water is really ok." She further explained to me, "That's probably why your veins are so flat this morning."

Finally on the third attempt, we had success with the blood draw, but you know what? All of this stress and suffering could have been easily avoided and prevented, if I was informed from the very beginning, that yes, FASTING means, no food and no drinks, but consuming water is perfectly okay. You see there's a valuable lesson here: when we as Humans leave off vital information or forget to mention the entire story – things turn out differently.

The stress that the young Phlebotomist was feeling and the suffering that I felt as the patient could have been prevented, if I had been properly informed that drinking water is acceptable, that it actually helps hydrate your veins.

So perhaps following proper "Protocol" is worth pursuing.

Exit . . . Stage . . . Left . . . Audience / Actors

What exactly does the theatrical terminology Exit – Stage - Left really mean? Is it referring to the actor's left or the audience's left? Which one?

It sure would look a bit funny, strange even, if during a live presentation, all the vibrant cast members were exiting off to one side of the stage, while you were standing all alone trying to leave the scene from the other side, unaware of the proper progression. Once again, dismissing, or showing very little aptitude for proper theatrical lingo could totally mess up a magnificent performance.

Sometimes "priorities" may seem small and so insignificant, but never underestimate their importance. You see, even though you may never appear on a Broadway stage, perhaps down the road, your grandchild may jump up into your lap and ask, "What does exit-stage-left mean?" Then, all of a sudden sharing that knowledge becomes your number one priority.

So perhaps following proper "Progression" is worth pursuing, if not for you, for someone else.

Awareness: Beyond Just Another Paycheck

Don Rutledge, a six time NCAA Final-Four Men's Basketball Official, not only inspired me, but served as a unique, effective teacher and mentor. He spent hours teaching basic basketball knowledge in the classroom, for which I am extremely grateful to have been a student. However, what I admire most about Don, is that he physically took the same principles and values he was teaching and applied them on the basketball court. Not only did he talk the talk, but he definitely walked the walk as well.

Likewise, Tony Maners an excellent NCAA Baseball Umpire, who has worked the College World Series in Omaha as well as being a solid Basketball Referee, had several opportunities to mentor me as well. However, this time around, the classroom turned out to be the actual gym floor during a live, highly contested Community College basketball game. Tony, the crew chief, had total AWARENESS that the head coach was getting the better part of my tail-end. So during a timeout, Tony walked up to me and stated, "Creighton, I need you to save your emotions. If this game goes into overtime, I am going to need your full focus and attention on making solid calls that can benefit this game, not on the colorful language that the head coach is directing and aiming at you, the rookie referee on the crew." Needless to say, I followed Tony's advice verbatim for the remaining minutes of the game.

You see anyone can be taught how to call a block/charge, balls/strikes or sign their job description, but it's those individuals who perform and respect their craft or trade, while at the same time, adding "Professionalism," "People Skills," and "Priorities" to the top of their game, who will excel.

Thanks Don and Tony, for sharing the entire lesson plan on what it takes to be a solid referee/human on and off the court. I am grateful you didn't leave anything out.

Up to this point, we have uncovered a lot of issues regarding the importance of prudent "Priorities." We've learned that "priorities" truly impact and play a vital role in all of our daily lives. No one is exempt.

In the 1940's, Abraham Maslow, an American Psychologist, helped define the process of establishing "priorities" through his simple five-tier pyramid, better known as Maslow's Hierarchy of Needs, which briefly explains that before Humans can excel, advance, or move toward obtaining higher "Prioirities," certain basic motivational needs must be met.

According to Maslow's theory:

Biological & Physiological Needs	Food/Water
Safety Needs	Security/Shelter
Belongingness & Love Needs	Family/Affection
Esteem Needs	Status/Achievement
Self-actuation Needs	Fulfillment/Personal Growth

Then as time marched on, yet another helpful discipline emerged called Project Management, where Engineers and Mathematicians worked jointly, emphasizing that "Prioirities" must be held to certain time restraints in order to optimize productivity. In other words, how can we effectively ensure that once these tasks or "Prioirities" are completed, it will strategically initiate the remaining "priorities" to start down the path designed for them?

So perhaps prudent "Priorities" and appropriate follow-through is worth pursuing.

Based upon what we have discovered so far, there's really not that much room for Hidden

Agendas or Personal Egos to set up shop or even dominate.

Recently, I was shown a staggering list of items that at first glance seemed a bit odd, but then as I looked closer and started to add things up, I realized that wow, word for word, that list actually prevents "Professionalism," "People Skills," and "Prioirities from taking root.

I am well aware that it's going to be somewhat tough for you to put down all your personal hand-held devices for a moment and focus on this troubling list. But, please do, because it's that important. We simply can't be oblivious any longer.

Please mark or highlight the ones that taint your thinking as well as weaken your ability to follow through with proper procedures, protocols and progression.

This list is quite extensive, so please give it your undivided attention.

PEOPLE WILL BECOME

lovers of self, utterly-self-centered vain
Lovers of money, greedy
Boastful, verbally arrogant
Proud, conceited lacking humility
Abusive, rude
Ungrateful, unappreciative
Without love
Unforgiving
Slanderous, insulting false accusers
troublemakers
Without self-control, loose in morals
Brutal cruel
Treacherous double-crossing
Rash acting without thought or
consideration
Conceited

Do you see how these behaviors disrupt or create the most damage to the people and things that matter the most to us? Can you see how these behaviors tear at the very fabric of all those beautifully written mission statements?

Don't Be Ridiculous: *I'll Run/Control My Own Life, Thank You Very Much*:

Who / What / Where / When / Why

With "priorities" playing such a major role in our daily lives, is it possible for us to truly spot and recognize <u>WHEN</u> Hidden Agendas / Personal Egos try to sabotage "Professionalism," "People Skills," and "Priorities?"

Take for example pre-recorded laugh tracks. <u>WHAT</u> exactly is the intent or purpose behind adding laugh tracks to sitcoms? Do writers, producers or the so called experts really think we as Humans need the assistance of laugh tracks to tell us <u>WHAT'S</u> funny or <u>WHEN</u> to laugh?

If in fact, the actor's one-liner was that wonderful or amusing, then <u>WHY</u> in the world would we ever need laugh tracks to influence our thinking? <u>WHERE'S</u> the logic?

So, <u>WHO's</u> really in charge here?

Soon after graduating from Concordia College, I remember quite vividly being confronted with that very same dilemma. WHO'S running or controlling my life?

For the first time in my life I was living on my own, no dorm buddies or parents around to give me a nudge or two. I was gainfully employed, so life was great, until reality set in over the weekend. Do I sleep and rest my weary bones or do I get up and attend a local church service? Part of me said, "Dude, stay in bed" while the other half of my brain was saying, "No you should probably go to church and start meeting some new friends."

After several minutes of tossing and turning, basically pondering and agonizing over my options, I decided to go ahead, get up, shave and shower. While toweling off, I remember feeling pretty good about the choice and decision that I made.

While en route to finding the nearest Lutheran church, I approached a slight incline on the stretch of highway in which I was traveling. It wasn't all that steep, so I proceeded up and over the hill driving right through a marked school zone, which just happened to be at the far entrance of the church parking lot. Well, about that time, I looked in my rear view mirror and noticed that I was being pulled over by a local police officer. At first, I wasn't too concerned, because I knew I was not driving all that fast, and besides, it was Sunday morning and I was sure the Officer would give me a break.

As the Officer approached my car, I could just tell by his body language he wasn't in any kind of a mood to hear my sob story or listen to a lame excuse. But in my defense, it wasn't a school day and there weren't any school children around. At least that would be my argument.

Well, guess what? I was handed a hefty fine for speeding through the school zone.

Believe me, at this point, I was extremely upset, angry, fuming to say the least. Not only did I get a stiff speeding ticket, but now I am late for church. I remember thinking sarcastically to myself, well so much for righteous "Effort" on my part. I mean this is totally ridiculous; I should have just stayed in bed.

As the officer politely drove away, I sat in my car for a moment trying to regain all my emotions and thoughts. But as I stared at the price of the citation, that's when "Analytical Thinking" began racing across my mind. As a recent graduate, where am I going to get the money to pay the fine?

I finally pulled into the church parking lot maybe 10 minutes late. I walked in quietly and sat in the very back pew. Then "Reasoning" entered the picture, and let me tell you, that's where things got really interesting.

Still angry and fuming on the inside, I bet I spent a good part of 20 minutes "Drawing concise Conclusions" on why in the future I might skip this weekly formality. However just prior to settling on that decision, I remember someone reaching out and tapping me on my shoulder, which was odd in itself, because I was sitting in the last pew. I remember turning my head and looking around, but no one was there. Then I heard this stern voice saying, "Jon Marc, first of all, let me remind you that you attend church to worship your Creator, not to simply socialize or network with new friends. Second of all, please quit your belly aching and fuming, because I cannot possibly come down from heaven and physically put my hands around your foot pedal and make you slow down through a school zone. That's something you are going to need to do. Listen young man, I love and care about you greatly, but from this day forward – you must learn to make "Intelligent wise Decisions" in all your daily thoughts, words and deeds."

It is no less realistic to expect our Creator to physically lift our foot from the gas pedal for us, than it is to expect harsh-speaking sharp tongues to tame themselves, or our eyes and minds from fixating on false or selfish ambitions.

In other words, while living on this earth it's our responsibility to lift or remove ourselves from any situation that is deceitful, whacky or deemed harmful.

Why, It's All Making Sense Now

Bucket List Our Time: A Precious Commodity
Flying by Rapidly

As our individual hour glasses fade away, it's not at all uncommon for many folks to create an authentic bucket list of things they want to do prior to passing away. Typically, it's a short, well-thought-out list drawn primarily from a set of unique, once-in-a-life time experiences, such as skydiving out of a plane, sailing around the world, enjoying a panoramic view of the world on a hot air balloon ride or perhaps visiting every major league stadium. But thank goodness, not all bucket lists have to be this lofty or outlandish. Many in fact are down to earth and quite practical in nature.

During a recent visit to Nashville, TN, while touring the old, historic Ryman Auditorium, I noticed a guitar propped up next to a microphone stand. Well, I didn't once hesitate; I grabbed that six string instrument, jumped straight up on that famous stage and belted out "Blue Moon of Kentucky" in the key of G. No exaggeration, my wife along with a few other shocked out-of-town quests witnessed the entire thing. So, standing and singing on stage at the old Ryman Auditorium can now be checked-off of my bucket list.

I do, however, have one more major item that sits at the very top of my bucket list. It's not so much about what I still want to do before shedding this earthly shell of mine, but more along the lines of what I'd like to share from my heart.

If you recall earlier there was a specific reference made about a Phlebotomist / "Patient" enduring unnecessary stress and suffering one morning, simply because some ***vital information*** was not shared.

I was the one on the receiving end of this three-needle-stick experience, simply because a few details were withheld. I'd like to now render some solid, valuable, ***vital information*** which potentially could prevent some unwanted stress and suffering from ever surfacing.

Remember earlier when you were asked to review or study that lengthy list of negative items that prevented Professionalism, People Skills and Priorities from taking up strong roots in our lives? Well, ironically that list is found exclusively in Second Timothy, Chapter Three, verses One through Five of the Holy Bible.[30]

But **understand** this, that in the last days will come perilous times of great stress and trouble [hard to deal with and hard to bear]. For people will be lovers of self and [utterly] self-centered, lovers of money and aroused by an inordinate [greedy] desire for wealth, proud and arrogant and contemptuous boasters. They will be abusive blasphemous, scoffing, disobedient to parents, ungrateful, unholy and profane.

[They will be] without natural [human] affection callous and inhuman, relentless admitting of no truce or appeasement; [they will be] slanderers, false accusers, troublemakers, intemperate and loose in morals and conduct, uncontrolled and fierce, haters of good.

[They will be] treacherous [betrayers], rash, [and] inflated with self-conceit. [They will be] lovers of sensual pleasures and vain amusements more than and rather than lovers of God. For [although] they hold a form of piety (true religion), they deny and reject and are strangers to the power of it [their conduct belies the genuineness of their profession]. Avoid [all] such people [turn away from them].

Oh my, are you picking up what's being laid down? Look closely at the profound, precise wording in these three paragraphs. It's like the writing is on the wall.

We as humans are going to experience an increase in ruthless behaviors. We can expect to encounter careless outbursts, fits of rage and senseless shootings.

The F-Bomb will become louder and much more aggressive. The Blogs and Tweets being exposed will be self-absorbed, damaging and demoralizing.

So what's our recourse? How are we supposed to handle this heavy load of "Worldly Wool" being pulled over our eyes? How in the world then, can we prevent this ungodly stress, pain and suffering from creeping into our lives and taking a stronghold on us?

Well, we've been given some very clear, direct and precise instructions in First Peter, Chapter Five verses Six through Ten:

Therefore **humble yourselves** [demote, lower yourselves in your own estimation] under the mighty hand of God, that in due time He may exalt you. Casting the whole of your care [all your anxieties, all your worries, all your concerns, once and for all] on Him, for He cares for you affectionately and cares about you watchfully.

Be well balanced, temperate, sober of mind, be vigilant and cautious at all times; for the enemy of yours, the devil, roams around like a lion roaring [in fierce hunger] seeking someone to seize upon and devour. Withstand him; be firm in faith [against his onset – rooted, established, strong, immovable and determined], knowing that the same identical sufferings are appointed to your brotherhood the whole body of Christians throughout the world. And after you have suffered a little while, the God of all grace [Who imparts all blessings and favor], Who has called you to His [own] eternal glory in Christ Jesus, will Himself complete and make you what you ought to be, establish and ground you securely, and strengthen, and settle you.

So, perhaps following this **vital information** is worth pursuing.

Another piece of the pie that is frequently left off or not even shared, is the fact that we Humans are quite similar to foolish sheep, in that, without proper guidance or direction we tend to stray and wander off course. In the small village of Gevas, located near the Van province in eastern Turkey, some 450 sheep actually fell to their deaths simply by following each other, one by one, off the cliff. Ironically, this occurred while the sheep were left unattended.[31]

It's no wonder why our Creator is adamant about us relying on Him as the Good Shepherd. John, Chapter Ten, and verse Eleven spells it out quite clearly when it says, "I am the Good shepherd." The Good Shepard assumes responsibility for watching over, leading, and protecting His sheep, even those who stray. The Good Shepard risks and lays down His own life for the sheep.

Proverbs, also known as the book of wisdom, drives home this idea of trust. Were you aware that in Proverbs, Chapter Three verses Five through Six, we are encouraged to *lean on, trust in*, and be confident in the Lord with all our hearts and minds and do not rely on our own insight or understanding. In all our ways know, recognize and acknowledge Him and He will *direct and make straight and plain our paths.*

Why . . . It's All Making Sense Now

So perhaps following the "Good Shepard" is worth pursuing.

No More Pretending / Sitting On The Fence

At this point, if you're like me, you are giving yourself an honest and private self-assessment. Facing our flaws, faults, and weaknesses is equivalent to admitting we are human. In order to embrace this notion of a wiling and loving Good Shepard, we have to adjust a little to the ways we've responded and handled the things of this world.

Sure it's bold, but the instructions found in First John, Chapter Two verse Fifteen is very specific, when it says; "Do not love or cherish the world or the things that are in the world. If anyone loves the world . . . then love for the Father is not in him."

Wow, once again, right to the point. As humans we're being asked not to be taking this stuff lightly or carrying around a lackadaisical, ho-hum, take it or leave it attitude towards our existence, our purpose and our helpful role while on this planet.

We can either hide behind our Bona-Fide Fool's mask, clinging to the pleasures of this woven

"Worldly Wool," or we can be obedient and become a wise Intelligent Decision Maker.

So, what's involved with <u>removing</u> this short-term mask?

Well according to Luke, Chapter Ten verse Twenty Seven: You must Love the Lord your God with ALL your heart and with ALL your soul and with ALL your strength and with ALL your mind: and your neighbor as yourself.

If you will, notice how many times the word ALL was used. What that tells me is that our Creator is striving earnestly not to leave any *Vital Information* off His caring instructions.

Wow, no one has ever mentioned this to me before. But how do I just turn my heart, my ALL to Him? How do I pursue love in this way?

Well, there is a guide in First Corinthians, Chapter 13, verses 4 through 8 that describe both what love is and what it isn't.

Love: is Patient, is Kind, gives no account of the evil done to it, rejoices when right and truth prevails, bears up under anything and everything that comes, is ever ready to believe the best of every person, endures everything [without weakening], and never fades.

Love is not: envious, boiling over with jealousy, boastful, vainglorious, haughty, conceited arrogant and inflated with pride, insisting on its own way, self-seeking, touchy, fretful, or resentful.

You see, it's no accident, no fluke that the strength and sole source behind our Professionalism, People Skills and our abilities to set and keep prudent Priorities come from our Creator.

Tragically if allowed the so-called "worldly wool" will attempt to persuade and program you into thinking that in order to obtain prosperity or to become comfortable in your own skin you must pursue a lifestyle of fame and fortune, acceptance, incentive plans, reaching certain quotas or cashing a lottery check.

But true sustainable wealth comes from our Creator. **... and here's why**

He has a way of helping us see and think clearly about such things, about all things. How is this possible? He is the Light. He illuminates those foggy, cloudy, shadowy areas of our lives and keeps us from tripping, slipping and falling. Try this:

Go stand at the entrance of your closet door. Be certain that all the lights are turned off and you're standing in complete darkness. Okay now walk in and reach out for your favorite navy blue socks or shoes.

Same scenario, go to your garage, with all the lights turned off, standing in complete darkness, enter and retrieve a ¾ socket wrench.

Well, how did you do? Were you able to find your way? Did you have any trouble seeing the navy blue socks, shoes or ¾ socket wrench while standing in complete darkness?

Okay, now this time turn around, turn on the light, walk in and reach right out for what you are searching for . . . Big difference between walking in darkness compared to walking in light, correct?

Why . . . It's All Making Sense Now

Jesus addressed a crowd by saying, "I am the Light of the World." He who follows me will not be walking in the dark, but will have the Light which is Life. (John, Chapter Eight verse Twelve)

So perhaps following the "Light of the World" is worth pursuing.

Constant Reinforcement / Relief NOW

I am not sure if anyone has ever communicated this **Vital Information** with you, but it's definitely worth repeating.

You see, our Creator truly understands that from time to time this ole world will play havoc and weigh heavily upon our hearts.

We are assured that: The Comforter Counselor, Helper, Intercessor, Advocate, Strengthener, Standby, the Holy Spirit, Whom the Father will send in My Name [in my place, to represent Me and act on My behalf]. He will teach you ALL things. And He will cause you to recall will remind you of, bring to your remembrance everything I have told you. (John 14:26)

Wow, isn't this reassuring information to know? Although what's even more astounding is how this same Intercessor will constantly restore Love - Joy - Peace - Kindness - Goodness – Faithfulness - Gentleness and Self-Control to those willing to follow His lead.

Seriously, we as humans can either hang or cling to the world's negative list that prevents personal growth or we can pursue the more effective and positive one.

Most assuredly, Love - Joy - Peace - Kindness - Goodness - Faithfulness - Gentleness and Self-Control are the exact ingredients that fuel Professionalism, strengthen our People Skills and solidify our Priorities.

In closing, I'd like to share a hand-written note that my Mother penned in my bible prior to her death a few years ago.

Dear Son –

This book has every answer to every problem. It is the only place you can go & keep your peace of mind, while traveling thru this world. Without it I would have perished.

I give it to you as the richest gift I can give, the only gift that makes any sense.

Read it, every time you have a chance & ask God to explain it to you, not Mom.

May you never dis-appoint [sic] its author.

Love Mother

References

1. U.S. Military
http://en.wikipedia.org/wiki/United_States_military_casualties_of_war

2. Schools

http://www.nytimes.com/2006/10/03/us/03amish.html?pagewanted=all&_r=0,
http://en.wikipedia.org/wiki/Virginia_Tech_massacre_timeline,
http://en.wikipedia.org/wiki/SuccessTech_Academy_shooting,
http://history1900s.about.com/od/famouscrimesscandals/a/columbine.htm,
http://www.foxnews.com/story/2006/11/09/university-miami-football-player-shot-police-rule-death-homicide/,
http://www.cbsnews.com/news/accused-shooters-of-nyc-hoops-star-tayshana-murphy-are-indicted-in-her-murder/,
http://www.huffingtonpost.com/2011/02/06/youngstown-state-university-shooting-fraternity_n_819268.html,
http://en.wikipedia.org/wiki/Sandy_Hook_Elementary_School_shooting

3. Elected Officials

http://en.wikipedia.org/wiki/2011_Tucson_shooting,
http://learning.blogs.nytimes.com/2012/03/30/march-30-1981-president-reagan-is-shot/?_php=true&_type=blogs&_r=0,
http://www.jfklibrary.org/JFK/JFK-in-History/November-22-1963-Death-of-the-President.aspx,
http://en.wikipedia.org/wiki/Assassination_of_Robert_F._Kennedy,
http://history1900s.about.com/cs/martinlutherking/a/mlkassass.htm, http://memory.loc.gov/ammem/alhtml/alrintr.html

4. Public Places

http://en.wikipedia.org/wiki/Westroads_Mall_shooting,
http://www.nbcnews.com/id/27957714/ns/us_news-
crime_and_courts/t/dead-after-shooting-crowded-toys-r-us/,
http://en.wikipedia.org/wiki/2012_Aurora_shooting,

5. http://www.apa.org/research/action/protect.aspx

6. http://depts.washington.edu/tvhealth/materials/third-party-
resources/TV-Children-Television-_Health-Development.pdf,
http://buy.cuna.org/download/27271_notes.pdf,
http://entertainment.inquirer.net/50596/government-to-crack-
down-on-sex-violence-on-tv, http://voices.yahoo.com/protect-
child-violence-television-829051.html

7. All State: http://www.makingafortune.biz/list-of-
companies-a/allstate.htm

8. State Farm: https://www.statefarm.com/about-us/company-
overview/company-profile/mission

9. Chick-Fil-A:
http://christiannews.christianet.com/1097585115.htm

10. NASCAR Foundation:
http://www.nascarfoundation.org/about-us/mission

11. Lowes:
http://retailindustry.about.com/od/retailbestpractices/ig/Compa
ny-Mission-Statements/Lowe-s-Mission-Statement.htm

12. The NCAA: http://www.ncaa.org/about/ncaa-core-
purpose-and-values

13. Southeastern Conference: http://www.secdigitalnetwork.com/SECSPORTS/THESEC/AbouttheSEC.aspx

14. Boys & Girls Club: http://www.bgca.org/whoweare/pages/mission.aspx

15. The First Tee: http: // www.thefirsttee.org/Club/Scripts/Home/home.asp

16. Joseph Institute: http://josephsoninstitute.org/

17. Girl Scouts: http://www.gshom.org/about/history.html

18. Grammy: http://www.grammy.org/grammy-foundation

19. Emmy: http://www.emmys.com/content/membership

20. Ben Davis HS: **http://www.wayne.k12.in.us/bdathleticdepartment/athletic _event_expectations.htm**

21. Homewood :www.homewood.k12.al.us/hhs/activitites/band/

22. NFL Play 60: http://www.nfl.com/play60

23. Papa John Pizza: http://company.papajohns.com/about/pj_mission.shtm

24. University of Georgia: http://www.uga.edu/profile/mission/undefined/?wmode=transparent

25. Notre Dame: https://www.nd.edu/about/mission-statement/

26. Virginia Common Wealth:
http://www.president.vcu.edu/ethics/index.html

27. USA Football: http://usafootball.com/#education

28. http://en.wikipedia.org/wiki/Isabel_Briggs_Myers

29 Observation Day, Week, Month:
http://www.epromos.com/education/calendars/

http://www.centredaily.com/2013/01/05/3455495/odd-observances-mark-your-2013.html

http://www.statesymbolsusa.org/National_Symbols/American_Hollidays.html

30. The Amplified Bible – Zondervan Publishing House:
www.zondrvan.com

31. Sheep:
http://usatoday30.usatoday.com/news/offbeat/2005-07-08-sheep-suicide_x.htm

About the Authors

Jon Marc Creighton is a native of Ft. Wayne, Indiana. He received His Bachelor of Arts Degree in Social Work at Concordia College in Seward, NE in 1982 and later earned his MBA from the University of Central Florida in 2010.

For the past 30 years, Jon Marc has enjoyed officiating the sport of basketball. Spending countless hours in the gym running up and down the basketball court has afforded Jon Marc the distinct privilege of observing Players', Coaches' and Fans' behaviors up-close and personal.

He started off simply officiating a few City and Church League games that quickly grew into Summer AAU games, the local Police Athletic League events and games at the Jewish Community Center. Eventually, after attending a few top-notch collegiate referee camps, Jon Marc began officiating not only at the Junior College level, but also at the NAIA, NCAA Division II and Division I levels.

Recognized for his communication skills, Jon Marc has been selected to work the FHSAA State Basketball Finals on a number of occasions throughout his career.

So, when Jon Marc speaks about there being a lack of Professionalism, a lack of People Skills and a lack of

Priorities, he has 30 years of first-hand experience to back that up.

****

Dr. Ursula Yvette Scott is an award winning educator and business woman whose work, advocacy, and contributions have changed countless lives during her 20-year career. Dr. Yvette is author of 40 & Fabulous: Forty ways to live your best days...after 40 and is a consultant and blogger at Allthingsyvette.com. She is the mother of 3 adult children (2 sons and 1 daughter) and divides her time between Central Florida and Atlanta, Ga.

To learn more about the authors or to arrange speaking engagements, visit 3one7mdedia.com.

www.ingramcontent.com/pod-product-compliance
Lightning Source LLC
Chambersburg PA
CBHW052154090426
42741CB00010B/2263

* 9 7 8 0 9 9 0 4 5 3 7 2 7 *